FINANCIAL PROOFREADING

FINANCIAL PROOFREADING

WHITE-COLLAR MIGRANT WORKER SERIES
NO. 5

GERALD EVERETT JONES

LaPuerta
Books and Media
www.lapuerta.tv

LaPuerta Books and Media is an imprint of La Puerta Productions, Santa Monica, California USA bookstore@lapuerta.tv

Trade paperback ISBN: 979-8-9860953-0-1
Kindle ASIN: B09Y12WW2S
EPUB ISBN: 979-8-9972017-3-9

This book is adapted from the author's textbook *How to Lie with Charts: Fourth Edition,* Chapter 13, "Financial Proofreading: Consistency Is More Than Its Own Reward," (LaPuerta 2018).

Cover image licensed from Canva.com. Photos by the author.
Cover and interior design by La Puerta Productions

CONTENTS

CONSISTENCY IS MORE THAN ITS OWN REWARD

A MAJOR PITFALL of business reporting is not only getting things wrong but also being inconsistent. So, mechanical correctness is a must, and it's largely a matter of editing — including checking and cross-checking to get things right — and enforcing consistency.

Proofreading? I know what you're thinking…

WHAT'S SO SPECIAL ABOUT FINANCIAL PROOFREADING?

These types of documents, which may be a matter of routine for you, often involve presentation or discussion of business results:

Types of Documents

- Periodic reports
- Management reports and analyses
- Letters to customers
- Narrative reports and white papers
- Presentations
- Email correspondence

Assuring the accuracy and reliability of this information goes beyond checking for mechanical correctness. And even at that level, seemingly small errors can be magnified in the minds of your readers because any kind of error invites criticism about the reliability of the rest of the document.

I haven't found a lot of resources on this topic. So I've included some of the issues I've encountered because creating financial documents has some unique challenges. And, like the issues that can arise when generating charts, ignoring these challenges can invite misunderstanding, give the wrong impression, or even imply wrong information.

Your business report or presentation's overall impression is a larger topic than just proofreading. It's not only about correctness — it's all about style. Style in a general sense is the kind of clothes you wear, the way you furnish your home, the way you set the table, and the arrangements you make for your wedding. But in English composition, *style* has a narrower meaning. And this particular meaning of style encompasses everything — about which there are *no firm rules!*

Now, there *are* style rules. But this can be a contentious topic because those rules don't always apply, and not everyone applies them the same way.

Let's just say:

Style is not black and white.

Large as the topic of style might be, achieving it comes down to enforcing consistency — which brings us right back to the tasks of editing and proofreading.

STYLE GUIDES

ONE BIG SET of rules is found in *The Chicago Manual of Style*. This book started out as a guidebook the University of Chicago made for its in-house press to deal with scholars and their publications. It rapidly became the bible for the book publishing industry. If you don't find the answer in there, nobody ever asked the question.

But we all know what happens when experts start making rules — they disagree. The other half of the publishing world — namely, newspapers, magazines, ad agencies, and public relations firms — use *The Associated Press Stylebook*, or AP Manual, which does not agree with the Chicago Manual on many obvious points, things that show up in your everyday writing.

THE SERIAL COMMA

An Important Point with a Twist

One everyday difference between the Chicago and AP manuals is the *serial comma* rule. Chicago wants a comma before the *and* (or *or)* in a series of items, and AP doesn't. Depending on which side of the Atlantic you hail from, this Chicago rule is also called the *Oxford comma* or the *Harvard comma.*

Here's an example of consistency winning over policy: When veteran journalist Bob Woodward published his book *Obama's Wars* with Simon & Schuster, he omitted the serial commas, even though the traditional rule in book publishing would be to use them consistently.

Punctuation and Style
Comma

"Serial comma*" rule
red, green, and blue (comma before *and*)

University of Chicago style
* also known as *Harvard* or *Oxford comma*

So which rule book should you follow? I think it's amusing that on the cover of the AP Manual, it says: **For journalists, students, editors, and writers in all professions.**

Not! Yes, reporters, publicists, and ad agency copywriters follow this guidebook to the letter. But most book publishers don't.

Nevertheless, whatever set of rules you follow, strive to be consistent. And, at the very least, stick to your choices within the same document. (As I suggest repeatedly in this book, keep track of your choices in your own editorial **style sheet**.)

If you have to comply with corporate standards or prepare documents for the public, you shouldn't stop there. An extra level of care is justified where financial reports are concerned.

Perhaps you were taught that there's only one way, one set of rules, and you have to follow those. If so, your teachers had a bias, however they were taught. But teachers who are covering basic composition often don't point out these options. Perhaps they don't want to confuse their students. Or perhaps they weren't taught that style isn't black-and-white.

There are many different sets of rules on style. To name just two organizations that differ, the American Medical Association (AMA) and the Institute of Electrical and Electronics Engineers (IEEE) publish guidebooks for editing scholarly papers in their fields. And these references disagree on many points.

Most companies, and all large corporations, have in-house style guides. And it's not uncommon to find different sets of rules within the same organization, especially if it's a large enterprise with many divisions or diverse product lines or is multinational. For example, it's not uncommon to find differing style guides for authoring aircraft repair manuals, annual reports, and advertising copy — all within the same company. Ideally, the company and its advertising and public relations agencies will decide on styles, and the agencies and department heads will help enforce them.

You probably know that the British have their own style rules, just as they insist on different spellings. And you can bet that organizations within the UK don't necessarily agree on the application of those styles. (A Canadian author once remarked to me that British readers will tolerate American style rules, but Americans are put off by British prose. So in his books he uses American spellings and style rules and sincerely hopes his British audience will forgive him.)

American style*

This, that, or "the other."

British style*

This, that or 'the other'.

*There isn't just one, but you get the idea.

In US English today, the Chicago Manual is pretty much the standard in the business world as in book publishing. However, if you're working in journalism, including writing for the Web, the AP is the recognized authority.

AMERICANS DON'T LIKE THAT BRITISH FLAVOUR (TWO EXAMPLES)

Here's another everyday difference between American and British styles:

A Common Mistake

- In accepted U.S. style, an organization is a singular entity – *it*.
  WidgetCorp today announces that it...
- In the UK, an organization is a plural entity – *they*.
  WidgetCorp today announce that they...

DIFFERING DICTIONARIES

THERE'S a dictionary in every office, although it may be buried in the back of the supply cabinet. Chances are, it's an old version and already out of date. For example, *workstation* used to be two words. Now it's uncommon to see it as anything but one word. As to *filename,* opinions are still divided. In IT, *filename* has been one word for a very long time. However, in general-purpose writing, you will often see it as two words.

What's changed?

workstation
filename or *file name*
podcast
mobisode
e-mail or *email?*

Here are some newer entries, culled from the bleeding edge of linguistic evolution: *Podcast* may not be in the edition of the dictionary on your desk, but everyone knows about it. What about a *mobisode*? It's a video episode designed for viewing on a mobile device, such as a smartphone.

Other emerging practices will affect your style choices: If you were to write *email* with or without the hyphen, you are not wrong these days. *E-mail* is considered more formal, and that's the way you'll see it in some dictionaries. Many people, including respected publications, use it without the hyphen, and these days I believe it's the most common form. Many other words often found in your business correspondence and reports — especially technical terms and jargon — are similarly evolving.

You will find an abridged style guide in the back of many dictionaries, covering some of the same basic rules from the Chicago and AP manuals.

And because these guides are written for general audiences, they typically try to have it both ways. Rules phrased like, "Some authors prefer…" acknowledge that style is not hard and fast. There isn't just one way.

After all, it's style. Is there a single dress code for work, no matter which company? Is there only one way to dress for a party?

STRIVING FOR PROFESSIONAL APPEARANCE

AGAIN, why bother with this stuff? It seems so trivial.

Whenever you make an appearance, and whenever you produce something in writing, you want it to be perceived as professional. And why not also — *classy?*

What are the elements of achieving that good impression? At a bare minimum, there must be no errors in content — no transposed digits, no misspellings, no wrong section or page numbers. That is, what you had in your source document should agree with what you show in your production document. (And if you find errors in the source document, check back with its originator before correcting them.)

But beyond having no transcription errors — and this is the real key to correctness — I repeat:

It's all about making choices and sticking to them — being consistent.

WHY IS CONSISTENCY SO IMPORTANT?

Here is the formula I would call a **dangerous equation.** I don't mean to alarm, but the consequences are not pretty. The scary thing is:

A Dangerous Equation

Inconsistency

equals

Perceived Sloppiness!

+

LACK OF THOROUGHNESS

ERGO

Mistrust of Your Results

!!! [YIKES] !!!

Any perceived lack of care begs the question:

How thoroughly did they check this report?

Or:

If I can't trust the smaller things like the way it's capitalized or punctuated, or the way my operating unit is abbreviated, can I really believe the numbers they're giving me?

ENFORCING CONSISTENCY

That's a huge punishment for sinning about literally small stuff, maybe only a few stray commas. But numbers have commas — and decimal points. Doesn't it matter where you put those?

So how can you strive to be consistent? What are the kinds of things to look for when you're going over these documents one last time before they are duplicated or presented or delivered?

PROOFREADING CHECKLIST

THE HEADINGS in this book can form a checklist for building your own editorial style sheet. Here are some areas of attention when proofreading and correcting your documents. I'll cover each of them in detail, with examples.

Areas of Attention

- Numeric consistency
- Footnotes
- Spelling and grammar
- Punctuation and style
- Appearance
- Accuracy

NUMERIC CONSISTENCY

PICK A FORMAT FOR REPRESENTING NUMBERS — and stick to it throughout the document. This rule is particularly important when showing dollar amounts. Elements of number formatting include:

- Truncation
- Thousands separator
- Small decimal quantities
- Negative numbers

TRUNCATION

If you have a column heading that omits thousands or millions, make sure that it is consistently marked, for example:

Numeric Consistency

- Make sure 000s or Ms omitted are consistent and clearly marked (*e.g.*, in a column head or in a footnote):

Net Sales (000s omitted)

$12,234 ***Same as*** *$12.234M*

In text, for round figures, you can use K for thousands:

$1K = $1,000

You can use *M* for millions and *B* for billions. (Oddly, the computer people use *G* for billions and the bankers use *B*, but that's just another stylistic divide that's not likely to be reconciled any time soon.)

- For round figures, use K for thousands, M for millions, B for billions:

$25.5 million should be *$25.5M*

THOUSANDS SEPARATOR

Always use a comma to separate thousands in monetary amounts:

- Use comma separator for thousands:

$1,485

This form is preferred over

$1.485K

for exact figures.

SMALL DECIMAL QUANTITIES

For amounts less than $1K, use the decimal point and add the two zeroes for cents, just so the reader knows you didn't accidentally leave *K* or *M* off the amount:

- For amounts less than $1K, use decimal for clarity:

$365.00

Otherwise, the eye will stop at the number in a column of larger figures and wonder why it looks odd. Similarly, in technical writing, insert 0 as a whole-number placeholder in quantities less than 1:

0.004 sec

NEGATIVE NUMBERS

The use of parentheses to show negative numbers is often inconsistent. Use curved parentheses, not the less-than greater-than signs:

(1,000) = –1,000

and is preferred instead of

<1,000>

which looks too much like

< 1,000

(If you get a stray space in there, you don't want the symbol misinterpreted.)

Minus signs also can be misinterpreted if there is any blank space between the sign and the digits. In general, it's not a good idea to use red text for negative numbers because red shows up as black on grayscale and black-and-white printouts. You might decide to use the parentheses as well as red, but then you're not strictly correct. Using red and the negative symbol (parentheses or minus) is a double negative, but you'll see it, and if done consistently, it's not necessarily incorrect.

- Use parentheses () to enclose negative values. To avoid confusion don't use <> or the minus sign, and don't intermix negative-value styles. If you use red digits to show loss figures in color outputs, also enclose in parentheses, since red reproduces as black on B&W printers:

(15,675) in red = -15,675 = (15,675)

FOOTNOTES

Financial reporting periods should be consistent. But if you grab financial data from corporate websites, from different customers, say, or from different reports, those sources could easily have *different fiscal years.* Any such discrepancies must be disclosed. Inserting footnotes is one of the accepted ways of explaining inconsistencies:

- Set guidelines on which accounting period to use as a data source:

  Footnote:

  3. All results are FYE (audited) except Tangible Net Worth, which is from most recent three-month unaudited period.

  Fiscal Year End (FYE)

Year-end results probably will have been audited. But portions of years not yet closed will be unaudited. So, right away, if you're consolidating multiple statements, you could be mixing fiscal and calendar year-end figures, or audited and unaudited results.

- Use a footnote to highlight any exceptional item, such as an unexpected or unusual result in a list of routine report items.

Sometimes you won't be able to avoid inconsistencies in narratives or charts that consolidate data from multiple sources. For example, perhaps you can't reconcile audited and unaudited results. And in some cases it may not be practical or even advisable to convert all monetary amounts to dollars since the exchange rate might have fluctuated significantly since the figures were generated. Or your source data may be inconsistent in some other irreconcilable way. But you do have the mechanism of footnotes to tell the reader what is an exception and why.

- Just as companies do in their financial statements, use footnotes to clarify and qualify sources of data, estimates or budgets instead of actuals, unusual circumstances, qualified auditors' opinions, differing accounting periods.
- In short, any intentional inconsistencies

Your organization's management will probably set guidelines on which accounting periods to include in a particular report. In general, use a footnote to highlight any exceptional item in a series of items, such as an unexpected or unusual result in a list of routine report items:

Note: These are mostly apples, but here's an orange.

Use footnotes to clarify and qualify data sources, estimates or budget figures instead of actuals, unusual circumstances, qualified auditor's opinions, or different accounting periods. In short, highlight any intentional or remarkable inconsistencies in the data.

In financial reporting, if the company has a relevant footnote in its financial statements, it may be advisable to pick up that footnote verbatim. It's usually wise not to rephrase it for legal reasons, so one of your proofing tasks would be going back to the source document to ensure the wording and punctuation match.

- If an item is footnoted in a company's annual report or SEC 10K, consider including the same note for that item in your report.

Discrepancies can show up in currencies and exchange rates or units of measure: dollars and euros, ounces and grams, oil and water. Those pairs don't mix.

- Make note of different monetary units

C$ £ € ¥

or exchange rates used for converting currencies.

Other choices you should make and then stick to involve your manner of presentation. For example, if you show a table to report one customer's results, you shouldn't show another customer's results on the next page in a bar graph. Perhaps you were in a hurry to meet a report deadline and pasted them from their sources because you didn't have time to generate new charts. But doing so is not only inconsistent, it's also confusing. You should keep to the same presentation format unless you have a very special reason for highlighting one set of results in a different way.

Consistency in document formatting extends to graphic design choices. Standardize on a font or a limited set of fonts. A good rule is to stick with one font for *body text,* also called *normal text,* and then use another font for headings (more on this later).

SPELLING AND GRAMMAR

I'M sure you know to use the spell-check function in your word processing application as the very last step before declaring the document final — and immediately after any subsequent revision. (You must know by now that "final" is rarely final.)

Spelling

- Use Spell Check in Word or Excel as a final quality-control step, after you've made all your edits and updates.

Spell-check functions in software typically flag errors in grammar as well but probably won't catch all of them. More robust checking applications, such as Grammarly, aim to be a timesaving aid for copyeditors. Nevertheless, as with the built-in spell-check, you should carefully decide on each recommended fix. **Accept All** isn't an option.

Spell-check apps seem to be getting smarter all the time, but be on the lookout for omitted words, as well as:

- Watch for misuse of correctly spelled words and sound-alike words (homonyms):

  their instead of *there*

If you need to consult a dictionary or thesaurus, here's a shortcut:

- As a quick check, try Google search:
  definition:*word*
- In MS Word, right-click a word and select **Smart LookUp** to use an online dictionary or thesaurus.

Use the software's automated spelling and grammar-checking features as a quality-control step, but nothing substitutes for checking it all carefully by eye. If you're in a hurry and don't want to consult the dictionary, keep a browser window open and search on the word, especially for proper, company, and brand names. Doing an online search isn't always reliable (depending on the source), so check a more authoritative source if you see discrepancies in the results.

ACRONYMS

Particularly in business documents, abbreviations and acronyms typically defy routine spell-checks. Here are some general guidelines:

- Use abbreviations mainly in tables and charts. Don't use them in narratives.
- Acronyms are exceptions. Spell out on first use if unfamiliar to your reader:

Cost Per Click (CPC)

Trademark™ or Registered® ?
There is a difference!

Other potential inconsistencies can be in the legends and color codes of a document's charts. Legends should show consistent names, spellings, and abbreviations for business units. Likewise, use the same set of color codes in all the charts. These types of errors will almost always creep in if you simply paste charts from multiple documents into your document.

ABBREVIATIONS IN SENTENCES

Using abbreviations within sentences is always a bad idea. An exception would be labels in tables and charts, when you don't have room. In those cases, use standard abbreviations, if possible:

Spelling

Abbreviations

- Abbreviate only where necessary to fit text in a small space. Use standard abbreviations and be consistent:

mgmt	*management*
add'l	*additional*
pgm	*program*
stmt	*statement*

In charts, tables, and figures, it is acceptable to omit periods after abbreviations. However, place a period after the abbreviation if the reader might not recognize it as such.

You can use acronyms in your sentences, but don't use periods with them and spell them out on first use:

The advertising rates for Cost Per Click (CPC) have increased steadily over the last quarter. Our ability to leverage CPC in the future will depend on our success at converting click-thrus to purchases.

An exception to using or not using periods with abbreviations is to follow legal forms for company or brand names, even if the form is not consistent with your style rules. For example, some company names use a period after *Inc, Co,* or *Corp,* and some don't. Again, follow the organization's accepted style, even if it differs from your house style rules. However, the abbreviations *LLC* or *LLP* never use periods.

PROPRIETARY NAMES

Also marked on first use would be trademarks — the TM symbol *Acme*™ — and registered trademarks — R in a circle *Acme*®. (There is a legal distinction between the two. Check the brand owner's site for the correct one.)

THE AMPERSAND (&)

Never, never, never use & in a sentence. The only exception is when it occurs in the legal form of a company name:

- Avoid using the & symbol unless it's in a company's legal name:
  XYZ & Co.
  or in certain common acronyms:
  R&D Research and Development
  P&L Profit and Loss

With the above exceptions, using the ampersand in a sentence is a mistake and always looks awful. And it only saves you two letter spaces over spelling it out. However, it's okay to use the ampersand and other symbols in chart labels and column headings, particularly to save space, especially when you're forced to use a small font (*e.g.*, 8pt) to fit a large table onto the page.

BEING CAREFUL WITH ABBREVIATIONS, ACRONYMS, AND COMPANY NAMES

If you have to abbreviate a word or a name, it should be an acceptable form of abbreviation, but it should also be abbreviated the same way every time you see it in the presentation.

- Follow the legal form of a company's name when using abbreviations. For example, some use a period after Inc. or Corp. and some don't. LLC has none. Some abbreviate Company as Co. and some always spell it out.

Corporate parent-child relationships can be a source of confusion. For example, you might start talking about Sears and refer to Kmart later. The two entities are parts of the same company now (as of this writing), but are you talking about separate brands or the same company? Kmart acquired Sears years ago, but Sears Holdings Corporation is the consolidated company. That's potentially confusing, and you shouldn't use the names interchangeably.

In another example, a credit report might consolidate data from several agencies or databases. Those sources might not necessarily be consistent in the names they use to refer to the companies — especially if the reporting period spans the time of a merger or an acquisition.

Check the corporation's website to see how it displays its legal and brand names. The best source is to click the **Terms and Conditions** link, if there is one, at the bottom of the home page. And certainly if the readers of your report are your customers or shareholders of that company, they will be very sensitive to the correct use of the name.

THOSE DISTINCTIVE COMPANY AND BRAND NAMES

Notice how these company names include unusual usage of capitalization and punctuation:

- Double-check company names and proper names, especially capitalization and punctuation styles of trademarks:

  Walmart
  Kmart
  Toys "R" Us
  Linens 'N Things

PUNCTUATION AND STYLE

AS THE DIFFERENCES between the Chicago and AP Manuals demonstrate, there are certainly rules about punctuation. And if you have a corporate style guide, there will be rules about style. However, applying style is usually more about being consistent than following objective rules.

Punctuation and Style

Sentences, Phrases, and Titles

- Begin a sentence with a capital letter and end it with a period, even if it is an item in a bulleted list.
- Don't put periods at the ends of phrases or headings just to be consistent.

BULLETED LISTS

The grammatical rule of *parallel construction* is:

When you have a list of items, you want them all to follow the same form, each presented the same way.

To follow this rule, edit the phrases in a list to be similarly composed sentences or fragments. That is, all lines are sentences and have periods, or none of them do.

Recommended
Bulleted List Style

- Do this first.
- Do this second.
- Do this third.
- Do this fourth.

All items same form;
all end with periods.

A formal style, which is becoming somewhat old-fashioned, is:

Alternate Bulleted List Style #1

- Do this first;
- Do this second;
- Do this third; and
- Do this fourth.

Semicolon after each item;
period after last item.

There are several other ways to handle bulleted lists, such as omitting periods at the end of each line even though the items are sentences, Even then, some authors insert a period only after the last item in the list.

Alternate Bulleted List Style #2

- Do this first
- Do this second
- Do this third
- Do this fourth.

Period only after last item.

Alternate
Bulleted List Style #3

- Do this first
- Do this second
- Do this third
- Do this fourth

No periods even
after sentence items

One very common way to distinguish between paragraph headings or bullet items is an **imperative** — to use the second-person verb form:

- **Connect the dots.**
- **Draw the chart.**
- **See the "Big Picture."**

In this case, the subject of the sentence is understood:

(You) Connect the dots.

Or use the **gerund,** the *-ing* form:

- **Connecting the dots**
- **Drawing the chart**
- **Seeing the "Big Picture."**

Connecting, drawing, and *seeing* in this example are nouns. So you'd put periods after the sentences, the imperative forms, but not after the noun forms, the gerunds.

SPACING AFTER PERIOD

In touch-typing class, they used to teach students to put two spaces after a period. That's not done anymore. The extra space not only looks odd in word-processed documents, but it also can also throw off letterspacing, particularly when you are using full justification, where margins are aligned both right and left.

INCOMPLETE SENTENCES

How can you tell whether to treat a group of words as a sentence or as a phrase? Yes, a sentence has a noun and a verb. But in this example, some of the words are understood:

Year-end results shown.

That's actually a sentence, or should be treated as a sentence:

Year-end results (are) shown (here).

TITLE CASE

If you decide to initial-cap all important words, that's called *title case,* the usual style for titles of books and articles:

The Chicago Manual of Style The Associated Press Stylebook

AMA Manual of Style: A Guide for Authors and Editors IEEE Editorial Style Manual

---

And if you use title-cased phrases in a bulleted list, you want to make sure that the same capitalization rule is applied to each phrase in the list:

- Mechanical Correctness
- Appearance and Readability
- Section Numbering and Pagination
- Indexing
- List of Acronyms

To recap, the following set of guidelines — although commonplace — is a mixture of rules and style choices:

Punctuation and Style
Sentences, Phrases, and Titles

- If a group of words is not a sentence but a phrase:
  - Initial cap the first letter and lowercase all the rest except for proper nouns:

    Year-end results phrase ***no period***

    Year-end results shown. ***[implied] sentence***
  - Initial cap all important words if the phrase is a title of something, such as a document:

    2015 Year-End Projection

SEMICOLON

You can use a semicolon to join two sentences, taking the place of *and.* You can also use it to separate major items in a compound list that contains both major and minor items:

Punctuation and Style
Semicolon

Main uses of the semicolon (;)

- Join two sentences, taking the place of *and.*
- Separate major items in a compound list that has both major and minor items:

  The combinations are red, black, and yellow; tan, green, and brown; and pink, purple, and blue.
- A good alternative can be *as well as:*

  The color scheme included red, green, and blue, as well as pastel shades of each.

A proper use of the semicolon would be in month-end reports to separate groupings of receivable subtotals. Accidentally omitting the semicolon or using a comma instead will be really confusing to the reader:

Correct

Past-due amounts: $35,456; 4,928; 103,453

Confusing

Past due amounts: $35,456, 4,928, 103,453

COLON

A colon can be used to join two sentences where the second one redefines or clarifies the first. You will find people disagreeing about whether the first word of the second phrase should be capitalized or not:

Punctuation and Style
Colon

Main uses of the colon (:)

- Join two sentences, the second of which defines or clarifies the first (means *that is*):
  One thing is certain: We will make our goals.
- Introduce a long list:
  red, green, blue, yellow, orange, and violet
- Introduce *very* long lists:
  1) long phrase, 2) long phrase, and 3) long phrase

HYPHENATION

Dictionaries and style books often disagree about the treatment of certain compound words. For example, some financial wizards spell the noun or adjective form *writeoff* as one word, and some hyphenate it *write-off*. But no matter which of those forms you use, if it's used as a verb, the correct form is two words.

Punctuation
Hyphenation

- Hyphenate a compound word used as an adjective:
  write-off period
- Unless the dictionary shows the word as always hyphenated, don't use the hyphen when the same compound is used as a noun or a verb:
  The write off will be taken in July.
  We will write off the batch in July.
- Check the dictionary on compounds that are now generally accepted as being one word:
  workstation
- Refer to corporate style guide for treatment of commonly used technical terms in your industry.

Other terms that have similar variations are *setup, followup,* and *breakout.*

APOSTROPHE

Here are some common mistakes with the apostrophe:

Punctuation
Apostrophe (’)

- *It’s* means *it is.* The possessive form *its* has no apostrophe (an exception to the usual rule).
- When making years or acronyms plural, do not use an apostrophe:
  - *CD’s* should be *CDs*
  - *1990’s* should be *1990s*
- Watch for “Smart Quotes” that go the wrong way. (Use Insert > Symbol command to fix):
  - *‘90s* should be *’90s*

However, when you use an apostrophe to talk about multiple letters of the alphabet, for example, it’s necessary to help readability:

Mind your p’s and q’s.

SMART QUOTES

This is more of a Microsoft Word thing: Those smart, or curly, quotation marks can drive you nuts, especially if you’re transferring documents between platforms such as PC and Mac or Word and OpenOffice. But also, if you just insert an apostrophe to indicate a contraction, such as *’90s,* Word is going to think it’s the start of a phrase, and the curl will go the wrong way. To avoid the problem, you can use the Insert > Symbol command and select the correct character.

APPEARANCE

YOUR COMPANY or your department should have standards for the appearance of documents. It gives a poor impression when sections authored by different workgroups use different fonts, margins, logo placement, and so on. Remember, this is the purpose of keeping a style sheet, especially if you don't have a set of company guidelines to follow.

Keep a Style Sheet

- Refer to and update your corporate style guide or department style sheet with new and unusual abbreviations and terms you find and are likely to use in the future.

Even if you're following the Chicago Manual, it can be a cumbersome book. (There is an online version.) It's handy to have a concise list of the styles and rules you often use. And, as a practical matter, once you make a choice, you might otherwise forget it by the time you've finished editing a long document.

PARAGRAPH AND CHARACTER STYLES

For a professional appearance, don't use multiple fonts in the same document, and be consistent about the styles you do use.

The Normal template in Microsoft Word has basic styles. For example:

If you start creating your styles manually, the program will add them as new styles rather than applying readymade styles (unless you turn this feature off). The result can be a mish-mosh. You'll have more attractive and consistent documents if you learn how to apply styles and keep them from multiplying like rabbits. Documents that have multiple authors and editors almost always have this problem. Good practice for a final edit is to reformat the entire document, using only the styles that you wish to appear.

It's good practice *not* to use the Normal style in Word for default paragraph text. That's because most, if not all, other styles are typically variations on Normal. Instead, create a new explicit style, such as **Report Body Text,** that is not based on Normal. Doing so will make it less likely that any redefinition of the Normal style in other users' Normal.dotx templates will cause the appearance of your document to change when they open it.

There's a practical reason to use heading styles correctly. When you insert a table of contents in Word, the application will only pick up those headings formatted with one of the heading styles. For example, if the topic is formatted as Heading 1, it will be picked up as a first-level topic in the contents. But if it's simply been boldfaced manually and changed to a larger point size, the phrase will be ignored.

TABLE LAYOUT

This example shows conventional style and format settings for tables that show financial results:

Left align leftmost column and text	Center column heads	Center column heads	Right align rightmost column and numbers
January	Text left or centered: Audited	Numbers right or centered: $1,000.00	$5,000.00
February	Audited	$1,000.00	$7,000.00
Use same number of decimal places in each row, so decimals always align vertically. Avoid intermixing data types in a single column.			

PAGE MARGINS

Also in terms of appearance, make sure your page margins are consistent. If the document is three-hole punch or has some type of binding, make sure you've added enough extra space, or gutter, on the bound edge. Microsoft Word provides these settings for controlling page margins and the gutter, or extra space along the spine for binding:

Margins and Gutter in MS Word

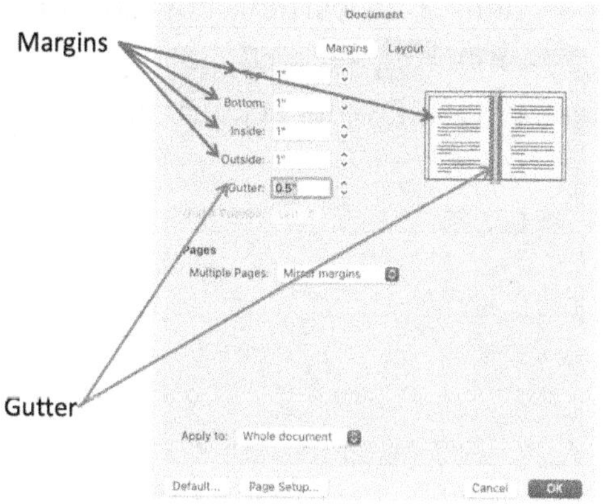

Try to apply consistent page formatting even if you assemble multiple documents from different sources. Resize pages to fit within your margins unless you absolutely must preserve the appearance of the original document.

- Make sure page margins, indents, headers, and footers are consistent from one page to the next.
- Don't neglect page numbering.
- Check for consistency and correctness of section numbers and nesting:
  - *1.1.1*
    - *1.1.1.a*
    - *1.1.1.b*
  - *1.1.2*
- Exception to the outline rule (an *a* must have a *b*): Don't renumber if you are following an official document, such as a Request for Proposal (RFP).

PAGE NUMBERING

Don't omit page numbers, which are not only helpful to the reader but also necessary if you're going to insert a table of contents. Page numbering can be tricky in Word, especially if your document has different sections. But learning how to insert section and page numbering correctly, along with headers and footers, is a skill worth acquiring.

ACCURACY

PROOFREADING TECHNIQUE

THERE ARE two basic ways to proof, one informal, the other formal. If you're proofing by yourself, the recommended technique is to look at hardcopies on your desktop. Use two rulers, one on the source document and the other on the printout of your report.

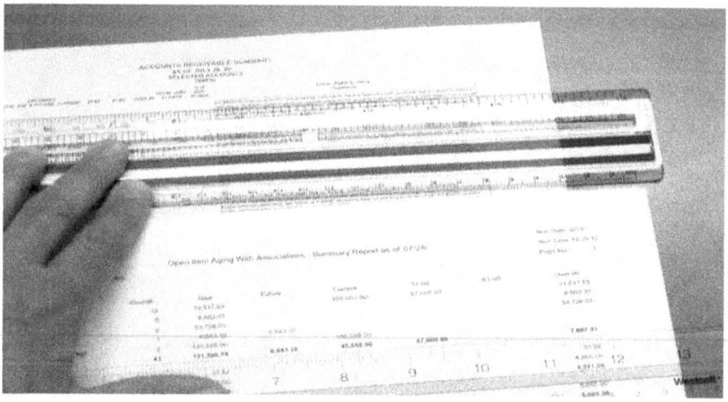

Accuracy

Informal proofing method for author's drafts:

One person at your desk

- Two hardcopies side by side
  - Data source and document
- One ruler on each to mark your place
- Some proofreaders recommend reading backwards to catch errors.
- On spreadsheet display, use Arrange Tiles to view two sheets side by side, row by row.

Proofing in the legal profession and in the publishing industry can be very old-fashioned. It takes two people, one to read the source document and the other to follow along in the production printout, noting the editor's or proofreader's corrections and markups, and spelling out proper names and unfamiliar words.

Formal proofing method for production

Two people (especially for numeric tables)

- One reads the data source aloud, including punctuation, and spells out unusual words.
- The other reads and checks the production document and marks any errors.

PROOFREADER'S MARKS

Even in this age of electronic documents, knowing how professional editors mark up printouts can be useful. Not everybody uses the same proofreader's marks, but it's important if you're working as a team to standardize on one set of marks.

Proofreader's Marks

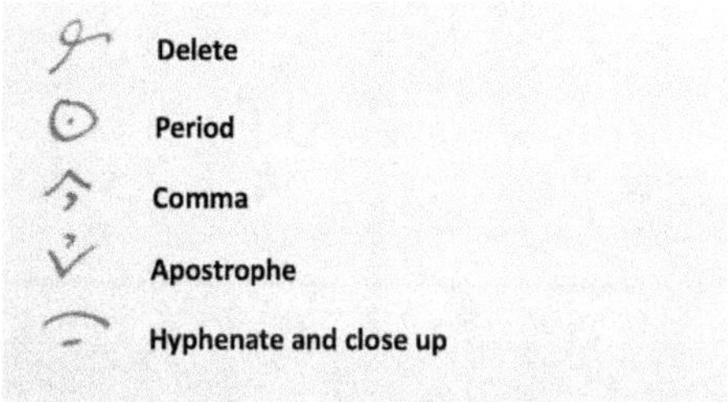

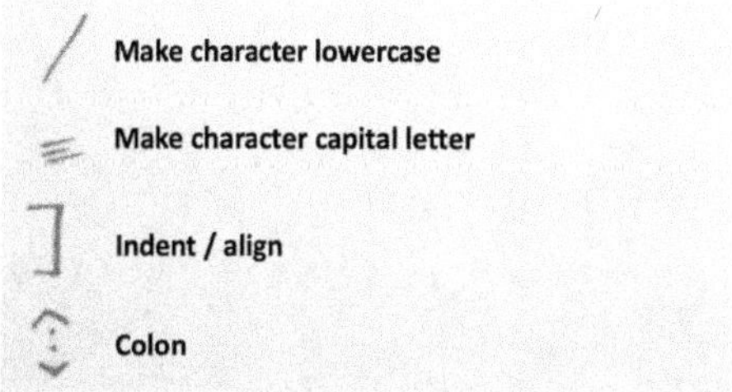

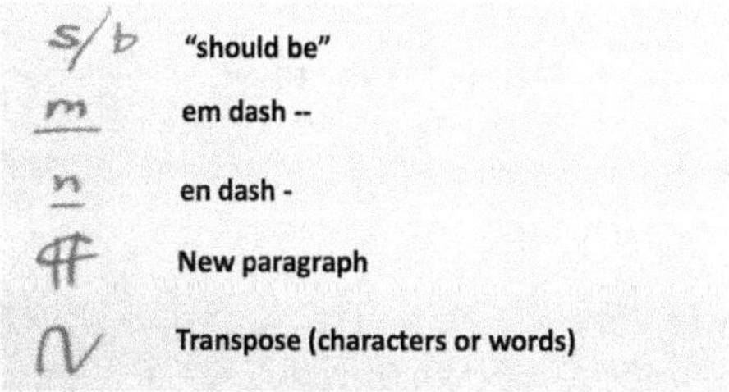

TIPS FOR EMAIL CORRESPONDENCE

EMAIL IS an informal medium and not subject to all the rules, but here are some useful tips.

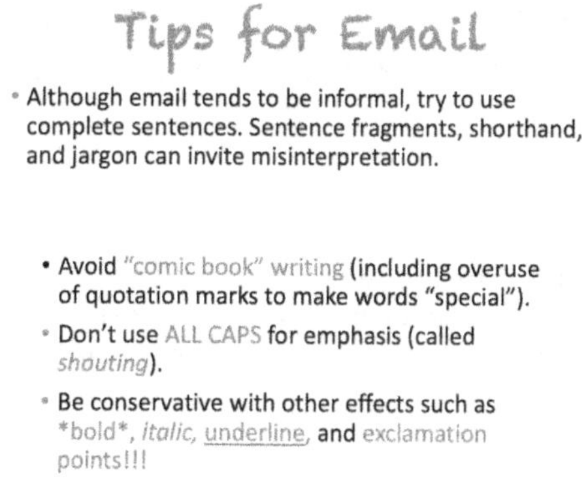

And if you want to be perceived as professional and businesslike, here's a tip for which I have no words:

In any business-related correspondence, be sure to document important names, dates, and events in your communications just as you would in a formal letter. Of course, the time stamp and the header information automatically do some of this for you. But, if a third party read your note, would they know what it's about? Granted, it's probably part of a message thread. But if you refer to "it," will your meaning be clear if the correspondence is reread a month from now? With just a few more words, you can set the record straight:

> Martha,
>
> It is nowhere near what we discussed.
> I have a real problem with it, and unless you can justify it, my supervisor certainly won't approve.

Here's an edited version of that same email that should make the sender's message clear to anyone who reads it:

> Martha,
>
> ~~It~~ The amount due is nowhere near what we discussed. I have a real problem with ~~it~~ the low discount percentage, and unless you can justify ~~it~~ your calculation, my supervisor certainly won't approve payment.

Use your auto-signature block if the correspondence is going to the outside. It provides your contact information, which is useful, especially if the document is printed out. The block should also have disclaimer language if your firm requires it and is particularly appropriate if the communication contains information that could be construed as confidential or proprietary.

When using your mobile device, your messages are likely to be concise, terse, and even cryptic. It's good practice, then, to confirm with a longer email or telephone conversation when you're back in the office. Start with, "As I mentioned in the very brief note I sent you from my mobile..." and then explain more fully.

FINANCIAL PROOFREADING GOALS

TO RECAP the advice in this modest book, checking your documents has two essential goals:

NO ERRORS

Your basic goal in proofreading is to make sure that the source documents and the production document agree, especially numerically. For example:

- Did we drop a digit?
- Are all amounts in the proper columns?
- Is there a human error that caused the documents to mismatch?
- Do the formulas in spreadsheets always generate valid results?

PROFESSIONAL IMPRESSION

But beyond correctness, you want the document to have consistency, which conveys professionalism. And it's not that the presence of consistency is drop-dead impressive. It's that the lack of consistency is so obvious and so obviously unprofessional.

You and your organization simply can't afford to look sloppy.

You want your reports to give the same impression as your best business dress.

Professional
and
Classy!

ABOUT THE AUTHOR

Runkee Productions

Gerald Everett Jones has managed major proposal and business analysis projects in government, healthcare, and commercial sectors. He is the author of more than 25 business and technical books on digital media production, including numerous how-to books on applications such as Microsoft Excel and PowerPoint. He has hands-on background in IT systems development and was project leader on the ARTIS computer graphics system, a precursor of PowerPoint. He has often led seminars on the topic of achieving honesty and clarity in business presentations.

Gerald is also an award-winning novelist, and he serves on the board of the Writers & Publishers Network (WPN). He writes the Thinking About Thinking blog on Substack geraldeverettjones.sub stack.com.

Reach out to him at geraldeverettjones.com and bookstore@lapuerta.tv

---

Gerald's Booklist

Fiction

Jonathan's Journal: A Novel
Harry Harambee's Kenyan Sundowner: A Novel
The Misadventures of Rollo Hemphill (#1 - 3): *My Inflatable Friend, Rubber Babes, Farnsworth's Revenge*
Mr. Ballpoint
Christmas Karma
Choke Hold: An Eli Wolff Thriller
Bonfire of the Vanderbilts / Bonfire of the Vanderbilts: Scholar's Edition
Clifford's Spiral: A Novel
Evan Wycliff Mysteries (#1 - 4): *Preacher Finds a Corpse, Preacher Fakes a Miracle, Preacher Raises the Dead, Preacher Stalls the Second Coming*

ABOUT THE AUTHOR

Runkee Productions

Gerald Everett Jones has managed major proposal and business analysis projects in government, healthcare, and commercial sectors. He is the author of more than 25 business and technical books on digital media production, including numerous how-to books on applications such as Microsoft Excel and PowerPoint. He has hands-on background in IT systems development and was project leader on the ARTIS computer graphics system, a precursor of PowerPoint. He has often led seminars on the topic of achieving honesty and clarity in business presentations.

Gerald is also an award-winning novelist, and he serves on the board of the Writers & Publishers Network (WPN). He writes the Thinking About Thinking blog on Substack geraldeverettjones.sub stack.com.

Reach out to him at geraldeverettjones.com and bookstore@lapuerta.tv

---

Gerald's Booklist

Fiction

Jonathan's Journal: A Novel
Harry Harambee's Kenyan Sundowner: A Novel
The Misadventures of Rollo Hemphill (#1 - 3): *My Inflatable Friend, Rubber Babes, Farnsworth's Revenge*
Mr. Ballpoint
Christmas Karma
Choke Hold: An Eli Wolff Thriller
Bonfire of the Vanderbilts / Bonfire of the Vanderbilts: Scholar's Edition
Clifford's Spiral: A Novel
Evan Wycliff Mysteries (#1 - 4): *Preacher Finds a Corpse, Preacher Fakes a Miracle, Preacher Raises the Dead, Preacher Stalls the Second Coming*

Nonfiction

How to Lie with Charts - 2020 Eric Hoffer Award Finalist in Business
The Death of Hypatia and the End of Fate
The Light in His Soul: Lessons from My Brother's Schizophrenia (with Rebecca Schaper)
Searching for Jonah: Clues in Hebrew and Assyrian History by Don E. Jones (Afterword)
White-Collar Migrant Worker (Series)

Related Titles

White-Collar Migrant Worker #1

Making Your Way in the Gig Economy

No job? Fresh out of school? Laid off? In the rapidly emerging gig economy, millions of workers will never have a job. But they can have a lifetime of profitable and satisfying assignments and projects. This handy little book will help you survive – and thrive – as an independent contractor. Don't wait for someone else to decide your future – here's how to write your own story.

Paperback or EBook

White-Collar Migrant Worker #2

11 Ways to Spot Fake News

Learn how to avoid misdirection on the information superhighway. Not to school hackers but to warn you, here are the most common ways someone can bend or break the truth to generate fake news. Many of these tricks rely on leveraging emotion to cloud logic. Another technique is to confuse cause and effect.

Paperback or EBook

White-Collar Migrant Worker #3

How Not to Abuse Metadata

No one need fear metadata or metadata analysis as long as it's summary-level data being shared. Unintentionally or deliberately using short-term trends or individual cases to generalize about the long term is a common pitfall.

Paperback or EBook

White-Collar Migrant Worker #4

Marooned! A Team Survival Game

In this team-building game, participants collaborate in small groups. A team score determines whether the team survives, and a private individual score helps participants evaluate their effect on the outcome.

Paperback (B&W) or
Kindle Print Replica (with color slides)

White-Collar Migrant Worker #5

Financial Proofreading: Not Amusing But Potentially Profitable

Learn how to make your financial reports both professional and classy. Diligent proofing in itself won't make a killer impression. But failing to proof for both accuracy and consistency could have woeful results. Perhaps numbers don't lie, but you can't afford a comma or a decimal point in the wrong place.

Paperback or EBook

White-Collar Migrant Worker #6

Technical Analysis Basics: Stock Market Charts

This coffee-break-short book will help you learn to spot trends in metrics applied to stock market price charts.

Learn the telltale characteristics of the Head and Shoulders chart pattern, along with how drawing its trend lines may forecast stock price highs and lows. Because Head and Shoulders can occur within short timeframes, it can be a useful tool for day traders and short sellers.

Paperback or Ebook

LaPuerta

www.lapuerta.tv **Santa Monica, California** bookstore@lapuerta.tv

The LaPuerta imprint and its logo – an open door – symbolize unlimited access to knowledge, opportunity, innovation, fascination, and delight.

Pitfalls of Business Reporting

How to Lie with Charts – 4th Edition

Eric Hoffer award-winning textbook used in college-level courses in data visualization.

If you're using a computer to generate charts for meetings and reports, you don't have to be taught how to lie – you're already doing it. Focus is on the principles of persuasive – and undistorted – visual communication. It's about careful thinking and clear expression. *Don't blame the computers. People are running the show.*

Paperback or Kindle Print Replica

This humorous novel is also a case study in entrepreneurship and the often zany world of consumer capitalism – inspired by a true story.

Mr. Ballpoint

Humorous Fiction (ages 14 and up)
Hardcover – Paperback – Kindle – EPUB - Audiobook

In 1945 Milton Reynolds introduced the ballpoint pen to the United States and triggered the biggest single-day shopping riot in history. Reynolds, an exuberant huckster who had already made and lost several fortunes, again became an overnight millionaire and then bragged that he "stole it fair and square."

Milton was a man ideally suited to his time—the post-war boom when the salesman was king and all of the rules had yet to be written. He was an old-fashioned, silver-tongued American peddler who would do almost anything—ethical or otherwise—to close a deal. His son Jim was a quiet honor student who couldn't tell a lie—even when he needed to.

Mr. Ballpoint is a father-son relationship story, told from Jim's point of view, about coping with Milton's outrageous schemes, then their sudden success. (It's a great Young Adult selection for book reports.)

"Forgotten history brought to life. If you ever wanted to know how to play the game of life and have a blast doing it, read *Mr. Ballpoint*. Perfect for our library and book clubs."

— **Deborah Vaden,** Manager of Libraries, City of Irving, Texas

"If only I had known about this marvelous invention before I started my writing career! No typewriter! No computer! The story calls to mind the old adage about pioneers and arrows. I salute Mr. Jones for his delightful and insightful tale."

— **Marvin J. Wolf,** author of *Rotten Apples: Tales of New York Crime and Mystery* and *For Whom The Shofar Blows*

www.ingramcontent.com/pod-product-compliance
Lightning Source LLC
La Vergne TN
LVHW050747061126
851857LV00013B/1033
9798986095301